Finances for Freelancers: Structure Your Business & Manage Your Money

Launching a Successful Freelance Business, Volume 2

Ashley Simpson

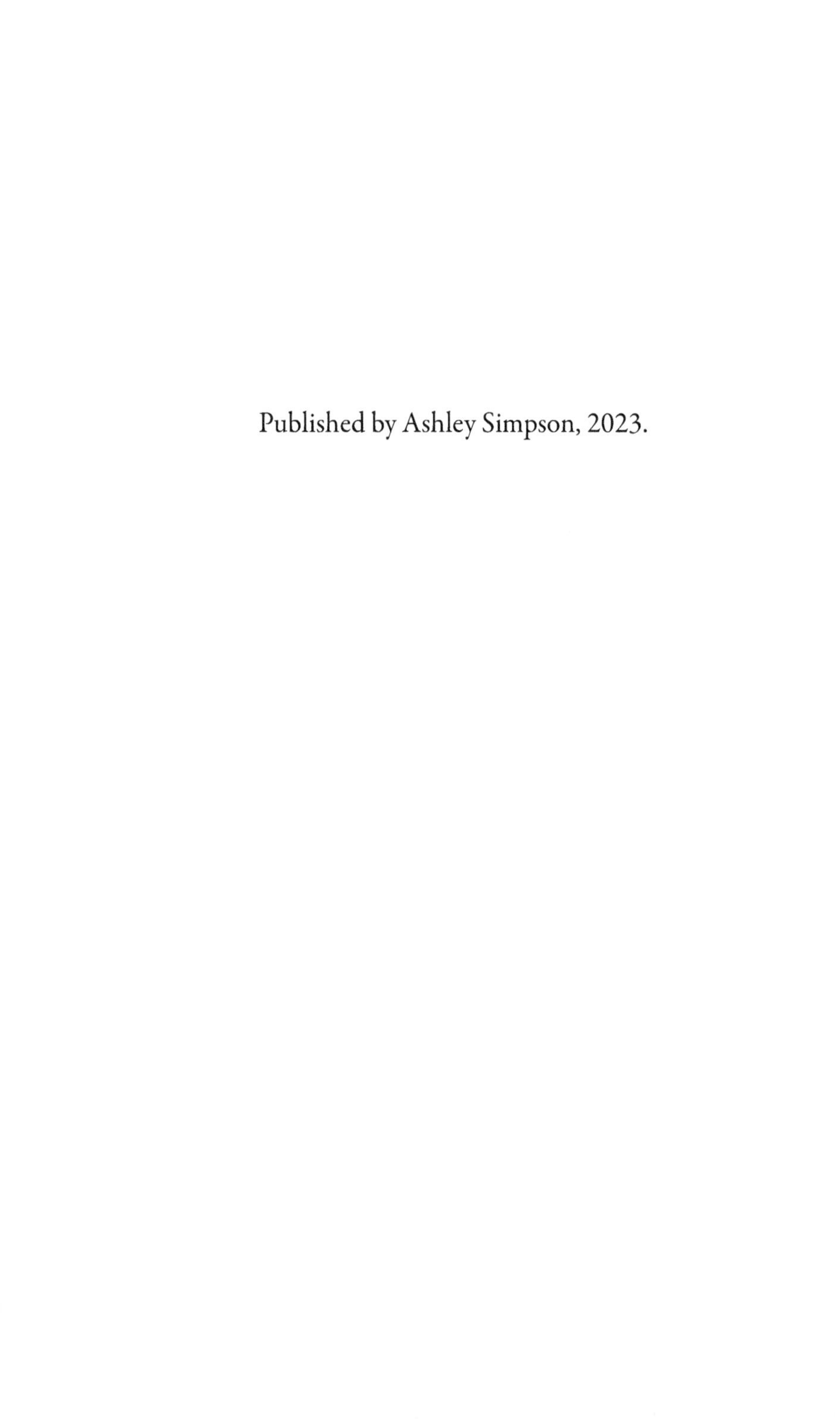

Published by Ashley Simpson, 2023.

While every precaution has been taken in the preparation of this book, the publisher assumes no responsibility for errors or omissions, or for damages resulting from the use of the information contained herein.

FINANCES FOR FREELANCERS: STRUCTURE YOUR BUSINESS & MANAGE YOUR MONEY

First edition. November 24, 2023.

Copyright © 2023 Ashley Simpson.

ISBN: 979-8223369455

Written by Ashley Simpson.

Table of Contents

Part One: Laying the Financial Framework

Maybe you feel ready to take the major leap into freelancing, but you want to ensure you have all of the prerequisites taken care of first. Freelancing is just as much a business as a retail outlet that sells t-shirts or any other good and service. This means you need to treat it just as seriously as you would opening a brick-and-mortar business. Preparation and understanding the key components of starting a business are essential to launching this new career. In other words, your freelancing business may not actually exist just because you say it does. It requires a little more planning and thought to make sure you can run a financially thriving and lucrative business for years to come.

There are certain items you must cross off your to-do list when you start taking on clients. The IRS is pretty firm about how businesses are viewed, and they want their slice of the pie when it comes to your income. It might not be the most glamorous thing to think about or talk about, but you'll be glad you spent some time thinking through the logistics of your business when tax time rolls around. In this book, we will cover the logistics of laying the financial framework to minimize the headache for you at the end of your fiscal year. From business structure to taxes, we will cover everything you need to think about when bringing on a reliable roster of clients.

When I first started freelancing, I had no idea all of the intricacies that went into starting my new business. I was on Upwork and just assumed the money I brought in belonged to me and me alone. I never gave a second thought to the IRS – until the end of the year rolled around and I started to think about taxable income. Fortunately for me, my business could better be classified as a hobby than a bona fide business in those early days. After all, I was making less than minimum wage on most of my projects. The benefit of being a broke college student is you have all the time in the world to pursue money-making and a little bit goes a long way when all you eat are ramen noodles. The IRS wasn't going to come for my measly thousand dollars earned over the course of the year, especially considering I probably lost money in the early days between buying equipment (a laptop and Microsoft Office don't come cheap) and from the fees rendered to the freelancing platform.

As I grew in my business, I found there was real money in freelancing and I needed to start taking my business more seriously. While I might have been able to get away without documenting my freelancing as anything more than a hobby in those first few lean years, I want something different for you. I believe you are ready to take the leap into freelancing because it will allow you the freedom and flexibility to live a life you absolutely love, spend more time doing the things you want to do, and be more present for your family and friends. That means you need to think of your freelancing as a business from the very start.

We cover mindset in my *Freelance Freedom* book, but we're going to take a different approach here – one that focuses more on the financial footing of your business. In part one, we're going to cover what you need to do to get your business off the ground. From choosing a business structure to setting up a business bank account, you'll get a clear picture of how to define your business and make sure you keep the taxman happy. Part two will show you how to manage your money as a freelancer who has to live through the feast and famine cycles. Both are essential to managing your new income source and making a solid living with a new business.

Whether you are thinking about starting a business to supplement your child's college fund or you want to make a full-time living with your skill and trade, this guide will give you everything you need to structure your business from day one. If you're ready to take the leap into freelancing, here is what you need to know about your business to make informed decisions. Let's take a closer look at where you should start: defining your goals and evaluating whether this is a hobby or a jobby.

Defining Your Business Goals

The first item on your to-do list might seem obvious: are you aiming to start a business or is this more of a hobby for you? The only way you can pin down the difference is by defining your overall goals and how you aim to achieve them. For example, some people will come to freelancing simply because they love the work and challenge of a specific project. They aren't aiming to make tons of money from this endeavor. Others are a little more serious about their business prospects. Folks who fall into this category are viewing it as an alternative to a draining nine-to-five gig. Even if you enjoy your full-time job, maybe you want to utilize your new skills to supplement your income so you can pay off debt or afford a new car. Start with the goals you have for freelancing in the first place.

Take a moment to list out every reason why you decided to take on this challenge. If the goals are monetary, you might need to decide whether this endeavor is going to be labeled as a real business or if it falls into the category of a hobby. The distinction clearly influences how you will ultimately proceed through the rest of this book. Hobbies require far less than businesses and may not require anything from you at the end of the year. Businesses are more complex, but they aren't impossible to handle on your own (or with the help of an accountant). For right now, simply think about your goals with freelancing. Write down everything you think you want to accomplish with this new career move.

Keep in mind that this exercise is different than the one we explored in my first book. In that exercise, we looked at the reasons why you might have wanted to pursue this as a career, including items like a flexible schedule or the ability to scale your income. Here, we are focused on the tangible results you hope to achieve with freelancing. If you want to buy a new laptop or a new car with your overall income, now is the time to write it down. The benefit of this exercise is that people who write down their goals are far more likely to achieve them than people who keep those same goals to themselves. There is something magical about committing your desires to paper that will allow you to form a plan that moves the needle forward on achieving them. Take a minute right now to write out your goals.

After you have taken some time to list out your financial goals for your freelancing, it should have become clearer to you whether this is something you want to pursue for fun or something a little bit more serious. The difference might require you to make the distinction between whether your new side hustle is a hobby or a real business in the eyes of the Internal Revenue Service. Here are a few ways you can determine whether your freelancing will fall under the purview of a hobby or a jobby.

First and foremost, the best criteria for determining whether your freelancing is a hobby or a job depends on how much money you make in exchange for your services. Hobbies typically don't make money at the end of the year. A good rule of thumb for determining whether freelancing is a hobby or a business is to look at the past few years' worth of income. The IRS typically states that a hobby becomes a job when it has turned a profit for at least three out of five years. The question is: what are you supposed to do when this is your first year of freelancing and you don't even know what you're going to be bringing in yet?

Sometimes, it will be easy to understand what the IRS categorizes as a job. Typically, these are skills that are deemed to be less fun than others. For example, a travel writer might love to take a trip to Florida so they can blog about it. Chances are, blogging about your travels is more likely to fall under the umbrella of being a hobby. Even creative writing can be viewed as a hobby because it's something many people find enjoyable and would gladly do without the exchange of money for time and services. On the other hand, you might be hard-pressed to tell the IRS that you enjoy some tasks. Collecting garbage isn't likely to be a hobby any more than filing tax returns is considered a hobby. Consider how enjoyable your work is and whether you would do it for fun, even if it didn't bring in the bacon.

Generally, the biggest indicator your freelancing is not a hobby is that you are engaging in it with the sole purpose of turning a profit. Even in the early years of your career when finances might be a little tight, you can tell the IRS your goal is to make money and chances are they'll believe you. Especially if this is a skill you have used to make money in the past (even at your day job), it is more likely to be viewed as a business. The same is true if you are employing a team of skilled laborers to assist you by opening an agency. Reflect on what your goals were in the section above. If any of them are related to relying on your freelancing income to pay your bills, then the odds are you need to start viewing it as a business rather than a hobby. On the other hand, it might be viewed as a hobby if you have another sufficient source of income that can pay your bills (often the case when you have yet to transition to freelancing from your full-time career).

The key thing to remember here is that income from *both* hobbies and jobs must be reported on your taxes. The difference is the form you will use and the amount of work required for filing your taxes. Hobby income is claimed in line 8J of your Schedule

1 on Form 1040. This is typically less involved than freelancing income. Freelancing income is filed on Schedule C of your Form 1040 and allows you to take deductions for expenses that can minimize your overall income. This is why it pays to keep detailed records of what you spend each year on your business. We'll cover more about what you can deduct from your taxes later.

The benefit to viewing your freelancing as a business is you can deduct business losses from your taxable income if you spend more than you make in the first years of your business. This can prove helpful if you have a full-time job and are spending more on the equipment and assets needed to run your freelancing business in the early days. Deductions reduce your overall tax bill and can even minimize the amount you will owe in taxes from your full-time career. Keep in mind whether your freelancing runs into the red too many years in a row. If so, the IRS may classify it as a hobby instead which minimizes the deductions you can take and could result in owing taxes on the money you claimed as losses during those lean years.

For most people who are pursuing freelancing and reading this book, the odds are you are looking to make at least a small profit from your services. When profit is the name of the game, you should always claim your freelancing as a business rather than a passion project. This offers you more protection in the event you get audited and can help you maximize deductions for items you had to purchase to get your business off the ground such as software or equipment. Once you decide your freelancing is a business, it's time to turn your attention to business structure to ensure you have the most advantageous framework.

With the last section out of the way, it's time to think about how your business is organized. I don't mean organizational flow charts that show a hierarchy of power in your company. For right now, we'll be talking about the *type* of business you intend to run. There are four main categories that most freelancing businesses fall into:

- Sole proprietorship
- Partnership
- Limited Liability Companies (LLC)
- S-Corp

Many of the documents required for each type of business structure will vary depending on your location in the world. Each state has its own guidelines for where to file, how to file, and what the requirements are for your business structure. We'll cover the most basic guidelines here and talk a little bit about the benefits of each one for you, your finances, and potentially even your team.

Sole Proprietorship

MOST FREELANCERS START their businesses as sole proprietors because it's the easiest way to get started. In fact, you might even automatically be funneled into a specific business structure if you choose not to do the paperwork to form one of the other business types. If you are the only employee in the business, then you will automatically be designated as a sole proprietor out of the gate. Because there is no paperwork involved in claiming your business is a sole proprietorship, this is the default most new freelancers will turn to for their structure. There are no state fees required to run this type of business, making it inexpensive to get off the ground in terms of initial investment.

Taxes are also relatively easy for sole proprietors. Instead of having to file a separate return for your business, everything is included on your personal tax return on Form 1040. Income from the self-employment of a sole proprietor is claimed in Schedule C where you can list out gains and losses for the year. This indicates how much you will owe on the taxes for the year (which should have been paid quarterly up until this point, but more on that later). You will also have to pay a self-employment tax on the money earned, so be sure to set more aside than you think. Just because your business structure is easy and clear doesn't mean you are home-free when it comes to taxes.

There is only one major downside to having a sole proprietorship: limited protection in the event creditors come after you. If a client sues you and you refuse to pay up, the courts can come for more than just your business. They actually have recourse to seize personal assets or funds in order to pay for your liabilities. The reverse is also true. If you have personal debts you haven't paid and a creditor wants to see their money, they can go after your business assets. There is very little legal protection for your assets if you engage in a sole proprietorship over an LLC or an S-Corp. It might be worth your peace of mind to file as one of the other business structures simply to know that your house, car, and savings account aren't on the line in the event something goes awry in your business.

Partnership

IF A SOLE PROPRIETORSHIP is the default for a business with only one worker (you), a partnership is the default for those who have more than one worker. Two or more people who are co-owners in the business form a partnership. Some business owners who work with a team might decide to draw up a written agreement so it's clear who does what and what share of the profits (or losses) belongs to each party. However, no written agreement is necessary and there is no paperwork to file if you want to run a partnership. Much like a sole proprietorship, the IRS will default to this type of agreement when you start your business. Keep in mind you will need to file a fictitious business name if you will be operating under anything other than your legal name.

Of course, it is worth noting there are some drawbacks to running a partnership. First, you don't actually own any of the assets related to the business – and neither does your partner. Instead, they are owned by the partnership itself. Every partner has a claim to those assets just like they have a claim to profit share. Everyone who earns a cut of the money should have a role in the management of the day-to-day aspects of running the business as well.

Also, you will not have any protection from lawsuits as we saw under the sole proprietor section. Protection does not extend to your personal assets unless you file for a limited liability company or an LLC (which we will look at next). One important distinction for this as partners is you are responsible for all business debt incurred by every partner included in the agreement. If someone else working in your business takes out a loan or purchases expensive equipment, you can be held liable to pay it back – even if you didn't know they took out the loan. Make sure you trust your partners to make sound financial decisions and have a system for talking about the finances within the company so you can all make decisions together.

There is also an extra step to consider when it comes to filing taxes at the end of the year, though it isn't as complex as it may sound. The income earned from a partnership is filed on Schedule E of the typical Form 1040 used for personal taxes. However, you will also need to file Form 1065 to provide information on the financial gains and losses during the tax year. This is the place where income, deductions, profits, and losses will all be recorded. One thing you may want to note here is that, like sole proprietors, partners don't withhold taxes from your pay. You will need to pay your regular income tax and self-employment tax on your earnings when you file your taxes.

Limited Liability Company (LLC)

MAYBE THE LAST TWO options sounded great in theory, but you don't really relish the idea that your personal assets could be on the line if your business attracts a lawsuit or if your partner takes out a loan you aren't aware of. The good news is there's a solution that provides you with some protection and it comes at a relatively low cost: a limited liability company (LLC). These allow you to operate as either a sole proprietor or a partner, but they form a completely separate legal entity that does not allow creditors to come after personal assets – no matter what. As a member of an LLC, you have the right to do all sorts of things to make your business run smoother such as opening a bank account, hiring employees, and even taking out a loan.

One thing to note here is that an LLC is comprised of members (either just you or you and a team of other co-owners).

Everyone invests money or services into the formation of the company, owns some share in the business, and receives a certain percentage of profits. Everything related to your agreement is written in stone and leaves no room for future conflict when someone is unhappy with their share of the proceeds. It affords everyone involved the same protection for their personal assets when an LLC is formed.

Forming an LLC does require paperwork which may vary depending on your state and can cost a small sum. However, the organization and protection it offers your business may be worthwhile for you. Usually, you will have articles of organization filed with the Secretary of State, a filing fee, and a state-mandated registration process. When you have a specific way you want to run the business, you may also consider filing an operating agreement or you can utilize the default rules set out by your state. There is a little flexibility in how you run your LLC. You will also have the option to take on a business name rather than operating solely under your legal name. Fees may be levied annually for your taxes.

Taxes for a limited liability company can be just as easy as they are for the other business structures we have already looked at. If you are the only member of the LLC, you will claim your business income on Schedule C of Form 1040, just like a sole proprietor. If your LLC has multiple members, you would file taxes the same way as you would with a partnership. This keeps taxes as simple as they need to be if you're worried about complexity at tax time. Some people will opt to be paid as employees of the LLC rather than as owners. A tax professional can help you file your LLC with the option of being taxed as a corporation or you could file as an S-Corp to begin with.

S-Corp

CORPORATIONS ADD A layer of complexity to your tax filings as well as require some extra funds to get started. Still, it's worth considering for those who are already making a full-time income with a freelancing business. In many ways, corporations are very similar to the limited liability company. Shareholders (a different term for those who are considered owners in an S-Corp) also have the same protection for their personal assets and resources. Business creditors can't go after personal bank accounts, cars, or even your home. At the same time, your business is protected even if you happen to incur personal debts.

Perhaps the most advantageous reason to consider an S-Corp in place of an LLC is the tax benefits. Particularly if you are the only owner in this business structure, S-Corps could lower your out-of-pocket expenses for Social Security and Medicare taxes. While filing for S-Corp status can be more expensive and more challenging than an LLC, it might be worth it. You'll be paid as an employee on payroll which can give you a more reliable stream of income for banks to look at if you want to consider applying for a major loan (think a home or a car). At the end of the year, your payroll company should provide you with a W-2 in the same way your corporate job provided you with a W-2 showing how much you earned, what you paid in taxes ,and any additional amount withheld from your check.

The only requirement is you must pay yourself what the IRS deems a "reasonable salary." If you need more money beyond your salary, you can take distributions that aren't subject to the same self-employment taxes as your regular income. Distributions shouldn't make up more than half of all your gross income, so make sure to do some research on what others with your job title make in the real world (and do some of the exercises in part two to see how much you need to make in order to pay your bills).

Not everyone will want to file as an S-Corp because it does have expenses associated with it: the cost of filing a separate tax return for your business, the initial startup paperwork, and the likelihood that you will have to hire an accountant to cross those T's with the IRS. You also need to pay a payroll company to process your paychecks. When should you consider filing as an S-Corp given the increased expenses? Most people will make the decision once they cross the $50,000 annual income threshold. Until then, it is likely worth your time and effort to consider one of the first three business structures included here.

How to Pay Yourself

The business structure you select ultimately influences how you will pay yourself, making it a key decision that should come at the very beginning of your journey into freelancing. After all, paying yourself is the only way you can survive in this world. Money makes the world go round, as the old saying goes. How do you ensure money hits your bank account every month so you can go about paying your bills and covering your expenses? In this chapter, we will take a detailed look at how payments work based on the business structure you selected in the last chapter.

Sole Proprietorship

A SOLE PROPRIETORSHIP is where many freelancers will start because it requires little to no planning to get your business off the ground. Instead, it serves as a default mode of running a business and anyone who wants to start a business of one qualifies as a sole proprietor. Fortunately, finances are relatively easy to figure out for this structure. Because you will be operating only under your own name, you can easily combine your business finances and personal finances. The money you make is solely your own and you can do with it whatever you please.

I recommend setting up a separate bank account for your freelancing income, but it isn't entirely necessary. The reason for having a separate business account is twofold: one, it makes it simpler to see exactly how much you're earning which is relevant for taxes; two, it makes it that much harder for you to take funds out unless you truly need them. You will have some money set aside in reserve for your overhead costs such as new equipment, subscriptions, software, and more. Unlike an LLC or an S-Corp, this separate bank account will still be a personal one though. It will just be set apart from your personal account, allowing you to transfer money back and forth.

The idea that the money you make is solely yours is appealing to many freelancers. If you make $100 redoing a client's website design, that is a tidy sum added directly to your bank account – but not so fast! Sole proprietors still have the burden of paying taxes and it can be quite steep. As of the time of this writing, the self-employment tax is 15.3 percent which covers both Social Security and Medicare. Chances are you never noticed how these taxes got paid when you had a traditional nine-to-five. In part, this is because you weren't responsible for the entire sum on your own. Traditional employers pay half of this tax and match what you put in as an individual. Without an employer to help you with your tax bill, you pay all 15.3 percent of it (though you can deduct half the cost on your taxes at the end of the fiscal year). With this amount deducted, you only have about $84.70 left of that $100 profit.

After you pay your self-employment tax, you also have an obligation to pay your regular income tax which varies based on your income. During the year that this book was written, tax rates varied from 10 percent to 37 percent depending on your income bracket and how you intend to file (single, married filing separately, married filing jointly, or head of household). If you are in the bottom bracket, you would have $74.70 left out of the profit. If you are in the highest tax bracket, you have $47.70 left over. Can you see how your taxes might eat into your profit quickly? This is food for thought when setting your rates.

Sole proprietors are set up for pass-through taxation which means all of the money you earn is going to be reported on your personal income tax return. Instead of filing a separate business tax return, your income and expenses will be accounted for on Schedule C of the standard Form 1040. Some people may try to keep more money in their business bank account at the end of the year, in hopes of avoiding personal income tax on it or as a means of saving up for an expensive purchase that could further the business in the coming year. It's important to note that you will owe taxes on *any* money your business brings in, even if you haven't transferred it to your personal account or spent it just yet.

Are you sweating thinking about the huge tax bill you're likely to face at the end of your year? For some people, this idea of paying thousands in taxes makes them feel queasy, but there's no need to panic. Self-employed individuals will need to pay estimated taxes based on what they earn and are projected to earn by the end of the fiscal year. In fact, you'll pay your taxes four times a year (known as quarterly taxes). The goal here is to help you set aside enough money to cover the entire tax burden at the year's end without tapping out your financial resources. These quarterly taxes go directly to the federal government and may prevent you from having to pay out of pocket when tax season rolls around. You may also need to file some state-specific taxes in the same way.

Partnership

PARTNERSHIPS WORK IN much the same way as sole proprietorships. If you are a member of a partnership, you will benefit from the same type of pass-through taxation as sole proprietors. In other words, your business will not file a tax return at the end of the year. Any money that was gained (or lost) during the year passes through the business and onto your personal tax return. Another similarity is you don't necessarily have to run payroll in order to transfer those funds around. Any time you or your partners need a little influx of cash to pad your personal bank account, you can simply withdraw money from the business account. The amount withdrawn is taxed at the end of the year, so make sure you set aside some of the money to cover your IRS tax bill.

Tax time presents unique challenges for partners. Similar to the sole proprietor, you will need to estimate and pay your quarterly taxes due in April, July, October, and January. These taxes go both to the IRS and any relevant state tax agencies. However, your tax return at the end of the year is going to be more complex than simply filling out a Schedule C on your standard Form 1040. Instead, you must also file Form 1065 to report income. The business will be responsible for filing Schedule K-1 to both the IRS and the partners involved to demonstrate the shares of each partner in the profit or losses of the business. This information is then relayed onto Schedule E of the Form 1040. It's a lot of extra steps, but the basic gist of taxes in a partnership is similar to sole proprietors, just spread out across multiple people.

Don't forget about those self-employment taxes either. The business itself doesn't match your contributions to Social Security and Medicare, which means you'll be paying twice as much as you usually did at a corporate gig. Normally, this money would be withheld from the paycheck so your net income would never even register how much you owe. However, you can deduct half of your self-employment taxes at the end of the year which will help minimize your tax burden. Make sure you keep careful tabs on what you owe (and what you pay) so you can maximize the deductions at the end of the year.

LLC

WHILE THERE ARE CERTAINLY great benefits to running a limited liability company, you won't find much help when it comes to paying yourself. Like sole proprietors and partners, you can withdraw money from the business bank account whenever the mood strikes you or in accordance with the agreement you have with your co-owners. This can be good news for those who don't want the headache or expense of managing a payroll company in addition to their routine business expenses. However, it can also muddy the waters of what you earn and owe taxes on at the end of the year. You'll have to keep detailed records of how much money you pulled out of a business bank account and how much you owe in self-employment taxes which still fall directly on your own shoulders. To stay on top of what you owe, the IRS mandates that LLCs must pay quarterly taxes as well.

If you are a multi-member LLC, you should have come up with an operating agreement at the start of doing business. This demonstrates who owns what share in the business, outlining how the profits and losses are distributed among business owners. The default is that if you own 60 percent of the business, you will receive 60 percent of the profits. This may not always be the case though. If it isn't, you can set up a special allocation to ensure everyone receives the payment for the services and goods rendered within the business. For example, you may want to pay more to your website designer than you would to the owner who merely provided the startup funds for equipment and training. While both have an important role within the business, one may justify a greater percentage of the earnings than the other.

There are a lot of finer details you may need to consider when registering your business as an LLC and paying taxes. For example, what you owe will be different depending on whether you are a single-member LLC (only employ yourself), a multi-owner LLC (taxed as a partnership), or if you elect corporate taxation benefits. Regardless of how you structure your business, you will still be responsible for self-employment taxes of 15.3 percent to Social Security and Medicare. State taxes will also apply depending on where your business is headquartered. These may be levied based on a sliding scale of how much income you earn or as an annual fee for doing business. You can find out what these state fees are by visiting your state's secretary of state site or calling to inquire with the Department of Revenue.

One thing to note here is not every member of the LLC has to pay self-employment taxes on their earnings. If you have someone who essentially bankrolls the operation but does not perform any of the work to keep the business afloat, they do *not* need to pay self-employment tax on their share of the profits. As soon as they step in to work or help manage the business, their share of the profits is instantly subject to self-employment tax. In other words, those who invest in a business for the potential return and don't intend to do any of the heavy lifting can minimize the out-of-pocket expense of the 15.3 percent self-employment taxes.

Keep in mind self-employment tax isn't the only money you owe to the IRS. Just like a sole proprietor, a partner, or any other type of employee, you also owe income tax based on the bracket you find yourself in. Freelancers who earn less might qualify for a 10 percent income tax rate while those who earn the most will be saddled with a 37 percent income tax rate. Plus, these numbers are subject to change annually, so you'll want to take a look at them early in the year to make sure you're on the right track to saving enough to cover the cost of your tax burden. As you can see, that

$100 made gets eaten up fairly quickly by taxes, so you'll want to maximize tax deductions (which we'll cover in a minute).

S-Corp

THE S-CORP HAS THE most flexibility when it comes to drawing a salary for yourself. There are three basic ways you can pay yourself: salary, distributions, or both. Most of the time, workers in an S-Corp are required to pay themselves a reasonable salary for the work performed. This means you need to do a little reconnaissance to find out what other professionals in your field are earning for the same services. Self-employment taxes are due on this reasonable salary drawn. This can be paid to you through a payroll company, meaning you will have a W-2 at the end of the year. For those who want the security of a "real" job and know they may want to finance something in the future like a house or a car, a W-2 is a great way to prove your income. You *can* still finance some of these items with another business structure, but it is harder to prove your overall income.

Once you have a reasonable salary established for yourself, you may sit down and realize you have more profits in the business than you thought. If you don't have anything else needing your attention financially like a new computer, high-speed internet, or some other software that could further your options, you might decide to take a withdrawal from the account, known as a distribution. The distributions taken are *not* subject to self-employment taxes which means they are essentially pure profit for you if you run your business this way. The catch is your distributions must be reasonable. You can't pay yourself a salary of 25 percent and then take 75 percent of the earnings in distributions to skip out on the tax bill. A good rule of thumb is your salary should be about 50 percent of your annual income or higher.

Because you will be on payroll with an S-Corp, you will not need to pay quarterly taxes in the same way you do with the other business structures. Instead, these costs will be taken out of the paycheck before it reaches your bank account. For those who want to spend less time when it comes to sorting out what they owe the IRS, an S-Corp might make the most sense. A payroll company like ADP can help you figure out what you owe the IRS based on your withholdings and can help hold you accountable for paying those taxes on a monthly basis with your salary rather than filing them quarterly.

Hopefully, this quick guide on paying yourself and the taxation of your business gave you a new appreciation for how much money it takes to keep the wheels on your business. You might be quite excited when it comes to collecting your very first paycheck for your hard work, but knowing how much Uncle Sam is going to take allows you to make smart financial moves. We'll talk a lot more about how to manage your money in part two, including how to make sure you have enough set aside to cover your taxes. For now, knowing that you *will* owe taxes on your income should be good enough to help get you started. In the next chapter, we will look at how you can reduce the amount of money you owe the government through tax deductions.

Tax Deductions

The good news is you can minimize what you owe to the Internal Revenue Service or your state government each year through tax deductions. These come off of your total earned income and do *not* require you to pay taxes on this amount. If you're looking for creative ways to lower what you owe to the government, you might consider how much you spend in some of these highly-used categories or plan to make an investment in some of these items to further your career while keeping more money directly in your pocket. Tax law is complex and changes from year to year, so you will want to consult with a tax professional to ensure these deductions are still viable for you and your business.

Self-Employment Tax

WHEN YOU HAD A REGULAR day job, you split the cost of your self-employment tax with your employer so that each of you paid 7.65 percent of your salary. This is one of the biggest drawbacks to working for yourself. You will have to pony up the money to cover the full brunt of your tax bill. While you may owe self-employment tax upfront on your quarterly taxes, you can deduct half of what you pay from your net income. In other words, the IRS views half of the money you spend on this tax as a business expense, allowing you to deduct it and capitalize on it to keep costs as low as possible.

Home Office Expenses

DO YOU HAVE AN OFFICE within your home where you do the majority of your work? Many people love the idea of working from home and don't want to spend money renting an office or sharing a coworking space. There is also a major benefit to working from home on your taxes each year in the form of a home office tax deduction. First, you need to tally up the square footage of the house as well as the square footage of the space used primarily for work-related purposes. This tells the IRS what percentage of your mortgage goes toward your workspace. Be aware they may audit your return if it seems like you are claiming an extreme percentage of your home costs, so be ready to prove that your office space is just that – a space where you exclusively perform your work.

There are two options for claiming your home office: a simplified option or the regular way which can influence what you deduct. The simplified version allows you to multiply the square footage of your office by a rate determined by the IRS each year. This is ideal if your office is less than 300 square feet. With this method, you can claim up to $1,500 as a deduction. However, you can also maximize your deduction with the regular method, calculating all of your expenses and the square footage of the home versus your office. It takes more time and recordkeeping to manage your business this way, but it could yield a better deduction. Calculate it both ways to see which way comes out in your favor.

In addition to claiming the deduction for your home office, you can also itemize expenses that power your home office. For example, you can write off the same percentage of your mortgage interest, home depreciation, and homeowner's insurance. You can even write off a portion of your utilities like electricity or high-speed internet used to keep your home office running. Even if you don't own your home, you can still write off some of the space as a tax deduction. However, you won't be able to claim as many of the deductible benefits like home depreciation because you have no ownership stake in the property.

There are also the items needed to keep your home office running smoothly. In addition to the home office deduction, you can also deduct some of the expenses related to your office like internet or phone bills. Your personal phone bill can't be deducted, even if you do use it primarily for business expenses. However, you can write off the costs of your bills if you have a second phone line dedicated to your business or if you have to pay exorbitant long-distance rates to call clients in other countries.

Health Insurance

ONE OF THE DOWNSIDES of working for yourself is you don't have access to a benefits package like many full-time employers offer. This doesn't mean you have to go without insurance though. Instead, you can find your own health insurance plan through the Health Insurance Marketplace at the end of the year (or during a special enrollment period) and write off the cost of your premiums for you, your spouse, and any children ages 27 and younger. As long as neither you nor your spouse have access to health insurance plans through an employer, you can write off the cost of health insurance premiums, dental insurance premiums, and even long-term care insurance.

Travel and Meals

DOES YOUR NEW JOB REQUIRE you to go on the road a lot? One of the perks of freelancing is you can work with clients all over the world – and you may even be able to travel to meet with them in person. Trips lasting longer than a single business day where you might be required to spend the night or rest qualify for a tax deduction. Not all travel can be deducted from your taxes at year's end, but those trips taken with the sole intent to conduct business are eligible. Valid business tasks that qualify for a tax deduction can include:

- Marketing or prospecting for new clients
- Meeting with existing clients about an ongoing project
- Taking a class that furthers your work skills
- Anything that involves work

Travel write-offs can include transportation costs like plane tickets or fuel for your car if you'll be driving to the destination. You can also deduct transportation in the city you visit if you'll be taking taxis, public transportation, or if you need to facilitate a car rental. Of course, your hotel stays and even some meals can be deducted as well.

Putting mileage on your vehicle, even without staying overnight in a new city, is also a tax-deductible option. You can write off mileage and gas expenses for trips you take in your vehicle, but you need to keep detailed records. You should have a notebook in the car recording the date, the starting and ending mileage on the odometer, and the reason for making the trip to prove it was for a purely business event. Many business owners prefer to take the standard deduction per mile from the IRS because it involves less recordkeeping. For 2023, the mileage rate is $0.655 per mile but this might fluctuate from year to year. If you kept good records of the miles traveled for business, it should be easy to multiply the total miles by this standard deduction to see what you can save on taxes.

Meals are a little trickier to deduct from your taxes at the end of the year and may draw a bit more attention from the IRS, so be mindful of following the guidelines. Travel allows you to write off meals while you're out of town, but it can also be deductible if you take a client out. The catch here is the meal can't be super expensive or extravagant, so use your best judgment when it comes to planning your meals out. The full cost of the meal isn't tax deductible but half of it is, so keep hold of those receipts to prove to the IRS exactly what you spent. You can't write off meals you take at the office if there is no business purpose associated with them. Even if you work while you eat, it won't qualify as a tax deduction.

Education, Publications, and Dues

PART OF BEING A BUSINESS owner is staying up to date on the latest trends in your industry. Education and learning should never stop, so think about what you spend on these items. Joining professional associations for your trade can be tax-deductible, as can any additional fees stemming from your membership to the organization. Make sure the organizations you join actually further the business though. Clubs that are designed more for networking or social exploration with potential clients aren't permitted as tax deductions. For example, a country club isn't a valid deduction because it does nothing to further your education. While it may be a great place to meet people who could one day become clients, you don't sign up for a membership solely to conduct business.

You can also write off the cost of educational resources such as trade publications featuring the latest news in your industry. Books, magazines, and more can all be considered tax-deductible if they are directly related to your line of work. Think about trade-specific publications such as Writer's Digest for a freelance writer or publisher. Books about marketing yourself or growing a successful business in your field are also great deductions. The catch here that you can't write off *every* publication. Just because you love *The New York Times* and it helps you stay abreast of what's going on in the world doesn't mean you can deduct it. It has to be focused on your area of expertise or business growth in general.

Education is a great way to invest in your business and it could be tax-deductible under the right circumstances. Continuing education must be related to your current line of work such as a class on search engine optimization for writers or logo design for graphic designers. This is a great way to advance your skills, open the door to more business opportunities, and become a more well-rounded freelancer. However, there's a catch when it comes to writing off your education expenses. Namely, you can't write off education related to something that doesn't directly relate to your line of work. Just because you're thinking of breaking into a new field such as web design doesn't mean you can learn about web design from start to finish on the company dime. Getting ready for a career shift is not a valid reason to write off an education expense.

Startup Costs

WHAT DO YOU NEED TO have in order to launch a successful freelancing business? Most freelancers have to make some kind of investment in their startup costs whether that means a new laptop, a set of programs that facilitate your work, or initial advertising fees. During your very first year setting up your new business, you can deduct up to $5,000 in startup costs which can encompass categories like attorney fees and accountant fees for getting your business off the ground. This is a great place to recoup your costs in filing for LLC or S-Corp status or any other legal fees you may incur. You can also deduct the cost of office supplies used during the course of the year (paper, pens, printer ink, etc.).

As you can see, there are tons of ways to reduce your taxable income, particularly during your first year of getting your freelancing business off the ground. The catch is that you need to keep detailed records of what and why you spend money on a given resource. At the end of the year, it will be far too late to start thinking about itemizing your business expenses and categorizing them for tax deductions. Come up with a system early on to manage your receipts and keep them on file. For the most part, I recommend investing in accounting software like QuickBooks for this purpose.

Another core component of managing your spending is to keep your business expenses and income separate from your personal income. In other words, you should open a new bank account that handles all of your business-related expenses. As a sole proprietor or partner, you can open an account under your personal name. It might be linked to your personal checking account for ease of transferring owner draws back and forth. This bank account should be where you have clients deposit your paychecks and you should always spend money on your business using a debit or credit card tied to this account – never your personal one. If you have a limited liability company or an S-Corp, you can open a business bank account for a small fee each month. This is a great and professional way to keep your business finances separate from your personal ones.

Make sure you choose accounting software that integrates with your business bank account. It will automatically pull in all of the transactions from your business, whether you're receiving payments or paying for a meal with a client. Then, all you have to do is select a category for the expense or income and it automatically compiles the data in reports like a profit and loss statement which can be helpful when working with your accountant to file taxes at the end of the fiscal year.

Of course, this is *not* a comprehensive and exhaustive list of what and how you can write some of your expenses off on your taxes at the end of the year. It is merely meant to show you the types of items and purchases that can minimize your expenses at year's end. If you have questions about what is tax deductible and how you can minimize your out-of-pocket spending, always consult with an accountant who understands self-employment and freelancing. As a bonus, look for accounting software that allows your accountant to see into your system. They can keep tabs on your business from afar and you'll always have access to their detailed advice about what you should do next to maximize your finances.

Benefits for the Self-Employed

Odds are you never really thought twice about the benefits you were offered at your office job. You had sick leave, vacation time, health insurance, retirement savings, and maybe even nice perks like an allowance for continuing education. Without some advance planning, those perks are all a thing of the past. If you want to take a day off from your freelancing business, there is no paycheck coming in while you lounge on the couch and watch Netflix. You need to keep some of the benefits in mind when factoring in how much you need to make to cover your costs.

Vacation Time and Sick Leave

TO BEGIN, YOU NEED to factor in how many days you might want to take off each year. Some people are used to having ten sick days plus ten days of vacation time. Sit down with your calendar and see how many days you plan to take off for the year, factoring in a little buffer room. If you intend to work as an hourly worker, you need to adjust your rates accordingly to make sure you can still pay your bills while taking some of this time off work. If you plan to take off (20) 8-hour days each year, this influences your hourly rate.

Here is how you can calculate an hourly rate: most calendar years have about 260 working days, but you intend to take twenty days off. This leaves you with 240 working days. If you need to earn $100,000 per year and you work eight-hour days, you need to charge roughly $52 per hour. You can adjust your hourly rate according to how much you need to make to cover your costs, which we'll explore more in part two on managing personal finances. The important thing here is to have an idea of how much you would ideally make and how many days you want to take off per year. This is a way of allowing you to take this time off without stress and allows you to have the same perks of an office job that might no longer suit your lifestyle.

Insurance

OF COURSE, THERE ARE other benefits you may want to keep in mind such as insurance. Getting your own insurance policy is easier than ever with the Healthcare Marketplace. Leaving a job should qualify you for a special enrollment period, allowing you to choose a new plan from a list of options organized by your premium (the amount you pay each month) and your copayments and deductibles (the amount you have to spend on medical appointments before insurance kicks in). The more you pay per month, the less you will have to spend on copayments and deductibles. Plans start at the bronze level with the lowest monthly cost, followed by Silver, Gold, and Platinum options that go up in price accordingly. Depending on how much you make and whether you have a spouse who is offered insurance through their day job, you might even qualify for a subsidy to offset the financial burden of paying for a health insurance plan. As we saw in the last chapter, paying for your own health insurance may also qualify you for some tax deductions, further minimizing what you have to pay out of pocket to the IRS at the end of the year. For more detailed information on how paying your premiums offsets your income, consult a tax professional.

Sometimes, you may be able to remain on your employer's health insurance plan for a short period of time, but be aware this will cost you. COBRA coverage is an expensive option, but it can buy you some time to explore other avenues of getting insured. Research and find the perfect solution for your budget. Typically, COBRA coverage is going to cost you the full price of your health insurance plan, which means there are no more subsidies from your employer which is what often makes the plans affordable and desirable. Instead, you will shell out the full cost of the plan plus a 2 percent administrative fee. In other words, COBRA plans are a great short-term option, but it will ultimately cost you. Stick with this method of insuring yourself for as little time as possible, using it to explore coverage through the Health Insurance Marketplace. You're more likely to keep a subsidized payment while self-employed in the Marketplace.

On the other hand, you might want to explore benefits like health insurance through other avenues. The easiest and most obvious solution is to take advantage of a partner's health insurance plan through their place of work. Oftentimes, this may not be financially feasible though. A partner might be offered a discount on their health insurance policy as a perk of working for the company which ultimately makes the cost more affordable. You might not enjoy the same discount which could price some of these plans out of what is affordable. If you are younger, you might even be able to remain on a parent's plan (even if they don't claim you as a dependent and you no longer live with them).

Depending on where you work and what field you work in, you may have access to health insurance plans through professional associations. The Freelancers Union is one such organization that can provide you with a variety of insurance options: dental insurance, life insurance, disability insurance, and even health insurance. It might cost you a small fee to join the association, but the benefits can be comparable to what you received via your day job. Local groups like the Chamber of Commerce may also have a group health insurance plan that you can join as a freelancer or a self-employed person.

Last but not least, you might qualify for Medicaid in the early days of starting a business. Your income may be unstable and considerably lower than what you earned at a day job, at least until you can get your legs under you with freelancing. Medicaid is available to low-income earners to help cover the cost of healthcare needs. Be prepared to submit your income documents and prove you make less than the threshold specified by your state. Income requirements will vary depending on the state, but a good rule of thumb is you could qualify if you make up to 133 percent of the federal poverty level. This varies depending on your state. Be sure to look at the guidelines for your state before applying for health insurance through other avenues.

Retirement

DON'T LET YOUR GOLDEN years suffer just because you no longer work an office job. Most people have no plans to work for the rest of their natural lives. This means you need to keep a careful eye on the horizon of your retirement. An employer might have made matching contributions and allowed you to contribute a portion of your pay each period to an IRA, 401(k), or some other type of savings plan. Contributions can still be made to a retirement plan once you transition to a self-employed lifestyle. You will simply have to choose a new method of savings. Consider consulting with a financial advisor to determine what type of savings plan is the right fit for you.

The first type of retirement savings plan you might want to max out is your IRA, whether it is a traditional or Roth account.

A traditional IRA is preferred if you want to reduce your taxable income in the current year and don't mind paying taxes on withdrawals in retirement when you may be in a lower tax bracket. On the other hand, Roth IRAs enable you to pay taxes on any new contributions right now and take tax-free withdrawals in retirement. If you will be in a higher tax bracket in retirement, Roth IRAs are the way to go. It's important to note here that the contribution limits for IRAs are relatively low at just $6,500 for 2023 (or $7,500 if you're 50 or older). If you want to make larger contributions to your retirement savings accounts, you may prefer a 401(k).

A solo 401(k) is ideal for those who have no intention of hiring an employee or who may work only with their spouse. The contribution limits are substantially higher than IRAs at a high $66,000 in 2023 (plus a catch-up contribution of $7,500 for those ages 50 and older). Alternatively, you could contribute up to 100 percent of earned income (whichever figure is less). Instead of having only employer contributions, a solo 401(k) also enables you to make contributions on behalf of the business. Employers can make contributions up to 25 percent of compensation before the tax filing deadline. Contributions to a solo 401(k) are made on pretax dollars and all of your distributions in retirement after age 59 ½ are going to be taxed. Once you hire an employee (other than a spouse), you no longer qualify for a solo 401(k) so think about other options if your goal is to scale or create an agency.

There are other options out there for self-employed individuals depending on how many employees you hire and how much you desire to contribute to your retirement. For example, a SEP IRA and a SIMPLE IRA are less popular options but may be the right fit for you. Both allow you to contribute more than traditional or

Roth IRAs and could be easier when it comes to maintenance over a solo 401(k). The point is there are a number of opportunities to save for your future, so this shouldn't be an area where you sacrifice when you make the transition to freelancing. Make sure you pick a plan that allows you to contribute without headaches or worry about the administrative elements. Oftentimes, this is best left to a financial planner who can offer advice, manage your investments, and handle the administrative needs of the different savings vehicles.

I highly recommend meeting with a financial planner as well as an accountant at the start of your freelancing business. This might seem like an unnecessary expense to incur when you have little to no money coming in at the start of your business, but it can prove to be an invaluable resource as you move ahead and start planning for your income and expenses. Plus, these meetings are tax deductible. Once you have your business off the ground, you should consider meeting with both professionals every six months to make sure you're on track for the year and are making the most of your benefits before tax time rolls around. At a minimum, you should meet with them annually to discuss new directions in your business, income changes, or a business loss that could impact your finances at the end of the year.

Overhead Expenses

The appeal of freelancing for many people is that it doesn't require much in the way of overhead. A brick-and-mortar business requires a commercial lease on a property, physical product, and even miscellaneous expenses like shelving and storage. To get your business off the ground, businesses with physical locations require greater overhead than digital businesses like freelancing. Still, you need to think about what your overhead expenses are so that you can budget for what you need to earn in your first few months or years of freelancing.

Overhead expenses are unavoidable for any business, but you need to factor them into what you must earn to keep the wheels on your business and pay yourself a worthwhile salary. Sit down and make a list of everything you need to get your business moving:

- Accounting software
- Professional memberships such as on Upwork
- Trade publications to keep abreast of changes
- Business bank account fees
- Payroll
- Continuing education
- Marketing and advertising your services
- Office costs or rental of an office
- Professional consultations with accountants, attorneys, etc.
- Travel expenses
- Equipment (including a computer and software)
- Retirement savings account contributions from the

business
- Internet or phone bills
- Filing fees for LLC or S-Corp

Overhead consists of any expense required to keep your business afloat. As you can see, most of the expenses on the list above don't directly make any contribution to your business. Typically, an overhead expense is money you must spend on services or assets that won't necessarily give you a direct return on investment. These items may be necessary, but they might not contribute to your business income. In fact, they can be quite a drain on your business finances. Try to keep overhead expenses to a minimum, especially during your first couple of years in business. Lower overhead expenses make it easier to turn a profit in your freelancing. Out-of-pocket costs will be low, which means that the money you make can be funneled directly into your payroll instead of back into the business. If you're thinking about making the switch to full-time freelancing, this ability to pay yourself from the beginning is essential. Over time, you will have more money to reinvest in your business. In the early days, you might want to simply focus on how you can keep money coming in to pay your personal bills as well as your business expenses.

Your overhead is directly tied to how much you need to earn in order to make this a viable business that can support you and your family. Sit down right now and list every expense you will incur in the early days of opening your business. Think about what you will need in year one and what expenses might be recurring in subsequent years. For example, you might pay for continuing education in your first year but let it fall by the wayside in years two and three because you have all of the skills necessary to perform your job to the best of your ability. Keep two lists, one for all one-time investments and one for recurring annual expenses.

This helps you identify the amount of money you need to bring into your business to cover your expenses and still pay yourself a generous salary. In part two, we will look closer at how much you need to make in order to cover your living expenses. For right now, it's enough to know you need to invest in some things upfront to get your business moving. Take this figure, add how much you would like to earn in a salary each year, and add your self-employment and payroll taxes to that figure. This should be your goal for business income. From here, you can break it down into your hourly rate, project rate, or number of clients you need to find to keep the wheels on your new business.

After you see how much you need to make in order to pay yourself, you may come to the conclusion that you'll never reach your goals. Minimize the amount you need to earn to pay your bills simply by slashing overhead expenses. Think about what is the most essential to growing your business. Chances are you can eliminate some expenses right off the bat such as getting a basic laptop instead of the most advanced option. Maybe you can work from home or go for a low-rent coworking space instead of renting an entire office. Marketing costs may be essential, but perhaps you could go for low-cost options like cold calling or reaching out to local businesses instead of relying on marketing materials. Travel might not be necessary in your first year of business which can slash overhead expenses significantly. As you can see, there are tons of places where you can save money on overhead expenses to make sure you earn enough to pay your salary. We'll talk a little bit more about how to slash personal expenses in part two, giving you a little more breathing room when it comes to the earning potential for your brand-new business.

Part Two: Money Management for Freelancers

Have you ever wondered what it takes to grow your freelancing business to the point where you have a steady stream of reliable income coming through your accounts each month? From the first moment you decide to call yourself a freelancer until the day you hang up your hat, you need to ensure your finances are in order. After all, you can only continue to pursue freelancing as a career move as long it's putting a roof over your head and food on your table. Everyone wants that regular paycheck that allows them to pay their bills, but being solely responsible for your income is a stress many freelancers aren't prepared for upfront.

Instead of having the steady guarantee of an hourly wage as long as you punch the clock, you might find yourself hustling to wrap up a specific project before the end of the month when your payroll is due. The benefit of this is you can certainly scale your income as much as you would like to, depending on how many hours you want to invest in your business. The downside is you are totally and completely responsible for your own livelihood. There is no such thing as coasting through life financially when you start your own business as a freelancer. Really, the moment you decide to call yourself a business owner, you have the ultimate responsibility for your own paycheck and the paychecks of any employees you might bring on to flesh out your team. The stress of managing your finances can be a nagging worry, never far from your mind, but know it's possible to find freedom from these thoughts with a little preparation and planning.

I know exactly how you feel. I remember what it was like when I first started freelancing more than a decade ago. When I took my first job as a freelancer, I was just out of high school and hustling my way through college with three other jobs. At my other jobs, I earned a steady income based on the hours I put in. Writing gave me the flexibility to work quickly and set my rates on a per-project basis instead of hourly. This allowed me to control the amount of time and effort that went into a project and ultimately helped me earn more.

I spent years grinding away at my business but was ultimately able to create a solid stream of revenue for myself and my family. We saved up and bought our first house, then our second. We were living the dream, but it didn't come without some significant effort on our part. Even with these external markers of having a successful business, I still had the mindset we didn't have enough money coming in to cover the cost of our expenses. What I really needed to do was to take control of our finances and tell them how to work best for me. I needed a system to tell me I was on the right track. That's right – I needed to start thinking about the dreaded B-word: budget.

I took a couple of personal finance classes and learned the ins and outs of establishing the fixed costs for my life, how to slash variable expenses, and why saving money for a rainy day is so crucial. It was a crash course in how to better manage my money, and it opened the door for me to start operating my business from a place of ease. Instead of hustling for another dollar all the time, I was able to rest assured that I had enough to cover my bills, pay for an unexpected expense, and still have enough for those items which are inevitable purchases in my line of work, like a new laptop or office supplies.

The bad news is freelancers often have uncertain income as their work ebbs and flows with the seasons. Fortunately, you can control for these leaner times with a little advanced preparation in your budgeting. If you are ready to start making the most of your money, this book will help you establish where you are right now, where you want to go, and what you need to do to get there. Stick with it and do the exercises at the end of each chapter if you want to really see the results of your financial planning.

It's also worth noting that you may want to bring on the help of an actual financial planner once you accomplish some of the tasks set before you in this book. They can help you make wise investments for your future and manage your money once you have a grip on where it's coming from and what you need to do to bring in more during lean times. You can make the most of an appointment with a financial professional by knowing the details included in this book. Whether you decide to make your own spreadsheet, use budgeting software like the ones we'll cover later, or stick with a paper-and-pen method, know your numbers from the very beginning and you'll be that much further ahead when it comes to opening the doors on your freelancing business.

Let's dive right in.

Freelancers are in a unique position when it comes to money management. They have the ability to scale their business to whatever level they have in mind, bringing in more money than is possible through a full-time position in an office setting that pays hourly. One of the perks of freelancing is you can call the shots on how much you want to make. Of course, you need to strike a balance between how much you want to make and how much time you want to invest in your business. That being said, there is one problem when it comes to managing your money as a freelancer: the business side of things tends to be a little hard to predict. Most people find that their finances fall into a feast-or-famine cycle.

Sometimes, the money will flow plentifully into your bank account and you will find you make more than you ever dreamed possible when you launched your independent business. At other times, you might find you have hardly any money rolling into your bank account. If this is the case for you (and it most likely will be at some point), then you need to know how to best manage your money. Here are a few guidelines to help you budget for both the feast and the famine.

Feast

WHEN WE SET UP YOUR budget, we will talk in more detail about what you should do during a feast phase of your business. For now, we will talk in general terms about some practices to put in place to ensure you have enough money when plentiful work starts to dry up. When you set your budget, you should settle on a salary you pay yourself regardless of how much money you bring in.

During the feast phase, you'll be bringing in more money than you need to issue this paycheck so saving it for a time when a famine rolls in is absolutely crucial. Nobody will stay in the feast phase forever, no matter how proficient they are at freelancing.

It can be tempting to start spending the money you have rolling in: maybe you need a new laptop or some fancy software to take your business to the next level. How do you decide when to spend some of your hard-earned cash and when to tuck it away in your savings account for a rainy day? I would argue you should keep a certain reserve in your business bank account to cover the cost of your salary for a little while, just in case work dries up altogether. Usually, I recommend letting your feast phases cover your salary for three months or so. The remainder can be reinvested into your business to enable growth or to take you to the next level.

The one thing you may want to spend money on right now is marketing. Like a game of chess, you should be thinking a few moves ahead. The time to market your services and put yourself out there is not when the work has dried up. By then, it's too late to try to drum up a little bit of business. You could be stuck in the famine cycle for quite some time and may not have any funds to invest in the marketing of your business. While there are free ways to find new clients (like submitting more proposals on sites like Upwork, which is free), you are much more limited when you lack the budget to spend on marketing yourself. Allot a modest budget for marketing in your feast cycles, and you'll find that you have work rolling in more consistently.

This is also a good time to set your long-term goals for your brand. Short-term goals allow you to figure out what you need to do in the here and now to drum up business. When you're in a famine cycle, the short-term is as far as you can really think because you are consumed with the need to acquire more work. Feast times allow you the luxury to think ahead a little further and start to define long-term goals (including financial goals). Know what salary you would ideally like to pay yourself moving forward, how many hours you want to work, and the type of work you would ideally like to be doing. Think one year, five years, and ten years out from this point. Because you have money rolling in at the moment, you have more freedom to ponder where you want to go.

Keep in mind the feast is just one part of the cycle, and you will inevitably come upon the famine. If you can adjust your plan during the plentiful harvest of your hard work, you have a better chance of making it through the famine without having to take on a part-time job at the fast-food joint around the corner to pay your bills. It may not be easy to think ahead for these cycles, but knowing what to anticipate and how to manage is key.

Famine

WHEN THE WORK STARTS to dry up, what do you do? The first and perhaps most obvious thing you need to do is tighten your financial belt and minimize spending. This isn't the time to invest what little bit of money you do have into new gear or technology. You need to make sure you have the money to pay your bills first and foremost. Keeping a roof over your head is essential if you want to keep freelancing. Slash as many of your expenses as you can: streaming services like Netflix or Spotify, grocery bills, and even your power bill are all variable costs that you could cut if you truly needed to. I would even argue that you should trim the fat on your budget *before* you hit a famine cycle, but we'll cover that in the budgeting chapter.

In fact, the only thing you *should* spend some of that hard-earned cash on right now is marketing. That's right – you should spend on marketing in every part of the cycle. Spending money on marketing doesn't necessarily mean you should blow your entire emergency fund (we'll talk more about an emergency fund a little while later). Instead, think about what free or creative actions you could take to bring more clients through the door. Chances are you can find a ton of free or inexpensive marketing options.

For example, Upwork has a free plan which allows you to bid on a certain number of job posts each month. If you upgrade to their paid plan (which is still relatively inexpensive), you get to bid on more jobs and can see the price ranges that other workers have proposed. The benefit here is you can ensure your budget is aligned with the marketplace.

Of course, you can also reach out to local businesses that might be in need of your services. Cold calling isn't for everyone. I know it causes my anxiety to skyrocket when I have to pitch myself to someone I don't know at all, but it can pay off big time. Even if they don't need your services right now, they may be able to refer you to someone who *does* need your services. Business people tend to be generous in their referrals, so don't hesitate to ask whether they know anyone else who might be able to utilize what you have to offer.

Ultimately, the best thing you can do to manage your money is to prepare for the cycles that will inevitably come. This starts with creating a budget that cushions your accounts for the times when you need to batten the hatches. Having an emergency fund padding your savings account or your business bank account is essential, but many freelancers (and solopreneurs, in general) have a hard time knowing what to do to make their budgets work. In the next chapter, we'll take a look at your budget as it is and how you can move ahead with a model that ultimately works for you.

Setting a Budget

With the feast and famine cycle in mind, you know the potential impacts to your income throughout the seasons. Start making your budget as early as possible when you launch your freelancing career and you'll feel much more prepared for what's to come. Even if your freelancing career has already started to take off, these exercises can prepare you for the future of your business. Budgets have a negative connotation for many people who feel budgets restrict them in their spending. They do keep you from spending more than intended in a given area, but they also allow you to have a greater degree of freedom from financial stress and insecurity. Before you take on your first client, I would recommend setting a budget as outlined in this chapter.

Before we get into the nitty-gritty of how to manage your money, let's define what a budget really is. Some people view it as a list of rules about where and how they can spend their money, but I view it more as a useful tool to get spending under control. Budgets are a great tool for you to identify what spending categories are most important to you, which ones are eating up too much of your money, and where you want to go into the financial future.

Instead of being a limiting tool that tells you how much money you can spend and where, they give you the freedom to spend on the things you decide will align with your values. If you want to get that cup of coffee at the café around the corner every morning, that is totally up to you. A lot of budgeting books will advise that you trim the fat on your budget so you can save more and even retire early. For some people, they don't mind working a little more to enjoy the small luxuries in life – and that's totally fine too. Nobody is here to tell you what matters most and where you should spend your money. With that in mind, here are a few categories you will need to consider when setting a budget for your freelancing business.

Find Your Expenses

ARE YOU READY TO START getting spending under control? It's time to figure out where the money is leaking from your bank account. I promise this first section is absolutely the hardest out of every step that comes in the rest of the book. Rip the bandage off here and now to gain the clarity you need to set your finances right. I recommend starting a spreadsheet with the data collected in this section because it can do the sums for you, but you can do the same thing with a pen and paper if you don't mind using a calculator. You will also need a copy of the last three months of your bank statements. We aren't going to mess around and guess at what you're currently spending – we are going to look at it head-on.

With your bank statements in hand, assign a color to each spending category. These might include things like:

- Clothing
- Restaurants and cafés
- Groceries
- Entertainment
- General shopping
- Toiletries or personal items

Take your bank statements and highlight each item in the color assigned to it. At this stage of the game, we are looking for your variable costs or the items that change from month to month.

Spend the most time identifying the categories where you spend money each month apart from your actual bills like rent, electricity, water, and the like. You'll notice that the list of potential categories above may not be completely necessary each month or you could trim them down some as in the case of groceries and toiletries or personal items. After you categorize your spending, punch each transaction into your spreadsheet or add them up to reach your total spending for each one.

Are you surprised at what you find?

Most people grossly underestimate how much they actually spend in the categories listed above. You might know you go out for Thai food once a week with your friends, but at $10 per plate, that's $40 per month. And that doesn't include the nights when you order pizza or even the groceries that might go bad because you're too tired to cook with the fresh ingredients you paid for at the grocery store or farmer's market. Entertainment is another big category where people tend to spend more than they realize. It isn't cheap to head out on the town for a night with your friends, even if you don't end up ordering dinner with them. Hopefully, this exercise gave you a little more clarity on where your spending is really out of control.

While you might be in shock at where your budget goes, there is good news to be shared. All of these expenses are variable, meaning that they can change over time. Now is as good a time as any to put a stop to this type of spending and start saving more. You may just find that you can leave your full-time job sooner and start freelancing more if you can slash these variable expenses by a small amount. For example, saving $40 per month on Thai food might add up more than you realize. If you make $10 per hour at your full-time gig, slashing the restaurant budget by $40 saves you four hours of work. Do this in enough categories and with larger sums of money, and you will quickly find that you may even be able to go part-time at your day job starting right now.

The hard part is you're going to have to stick with these spending cuts long-term while you get your business off the ground. Explaining to your friends you can't go out with them is hard, but you can suggest new options that come in at a lower overall cost. Maybe you could stay home and watch a movie on Netflix with homemade popcorn instead of heading to the theater where you would usually drop $30 or $40 per movie. Because we've already seen that freelancing tends to favor feast-or-famine cycles, you don't want to increase your spending just because you have a very good month. You can reward yourself with something small for a job well done like maybe a single night out. However, you don't want to make drastic decisions in your budget which could leave you strapped during a month when the famine hits.

At this point in the process, it's time to decide where you actually *want* your money to go each month. With the numbers spread out before you, it's much easier to figure out where your top priorities are when it comes to spending. If a sense of community is a major source of joy in your life, then you may not want to cut out the entertainment you do with friends. Maybe you know it isn't realistic for you to eat every meal at home, so you create a small fund for dining out just once or twice each week. The idea here isn't to slash every expense possible down to zero. If you haven't been living frugally already, it would be unrealistic to think about cutting every one of your expenses down to the bone.

That being said, there might come a time when you actually *do* have to cut out all of these extraneous categories of spending. When you first make the leap into freelancing full-time, clients may be few and far between. It's more than possible to run a successful career with a rotation of high-paying clients, but it won't happen overnight. Quitting your full-time job in order to move to freelancing without having any clients lined up can be a major financial emergency. Setting aside some money in savings for your runway is essential, but you don't want to gobble up your runway with frivolous spending. Evaluate the more realistic budget cuts that might feel sacrificial to you without depriving you of real joy. If it is truly important to you, then you might want to find a way to keep it in your budget even if it means staying a little longer at your full-time job or taking on an extra client to afford those luxuries.

If you have done this work, then it's time to commit to paper. You can use the accompanying notebook I designed for freelancers to keep track of your spending categories or create a spreadsheet using programs like Google Sheets or Microsoft Excel. Come up with labels for the categories where you intend to keep variable expenses: food, dining out, entertainment, clothing, and so on. Write down what you are currently spending on these expenses alongside a new, revised number so you know the target to aim for. We'll talk more about how to ensure you don't exceed this number in a later chapter. For now, you are simply doing the heavy lifting of refining your spending habits and figuring out what is realistic for you. Tally up your new numbers and see exactly what you are aiming to spend so you can start to get a big-picture idea of what you need to earn to support your lifestyle.

Fixed Costs

FORTUNATELY, THE VARIABLE costs of your lifestyle are the hardest part to track. If you made it through that last section without tears, then this section will be a breeze in comparison.

Variable costs are those that can fluctuate from month to month, but your fixed costs often comprise a greater portion of your monthly budget. Fixed costs never change from month to month so they're quite easy to plan for and anticipate in the creation of a budget. A fixed cost is something like your rent, water bill, or pest control services. Maybe you have a car payment that comes out of your bank account every month.

If you have a bill to pay that never changes month after month, it falls under the umbrella of fixed costs. Feel free to take another look at your bank statements with a new color. Circle or highlight everything that you pay monthly that never changes. Then, go through the same process of tallying up all of those expenses to see what your total spending is. Chances are you have a good idea of what these items cost you, but you may have never looked at them holistically like this. Add up your numbers and then combine them with your variable cost estimates to see what you need to cover all of your bills at the end of each month. It might be a big number, but hold tight before you panic.

For those who have never set a budget, figuring out what you realistically spend each month might be a sobering activity. It might even feel discouraging to see that number add up and think you will never be able to earn enough via freelancing to support yourself. I'm here to tell you it is *more* than possible to earn a decent living freelancing and to support yourself this way. I have been doing it for more than a decade. Times were lean when I first started freelancing full-time, but we tightened our metaphorical coin pouches and slashed spending while I built up a roster of reliable clients. You can do this too, but it will take some time. Maybe it means you need to stay at a full-time job a little while longer until you can cover half of your expenses with freelancing.

Perhaps you need to take on another part-time job or scale back your current career to make room for freelancing. Do what works for you, but know that it's possible to earn four or even five figures every month through your freelance work.

Keep in mind your fixed costs don't necessarily have to be "fixed." One way you might be able to justify shifting into freelancing is by cutting back on those fixed costs. The most obvious way to save money could be to find a new and less expensive place to live. Rent or even a mortgage tends to be the highest expense on most budgets. Living in a luxury apartment home or a house that exceeds your means puts a serious strain on your finances. Consider what you may save by moving and determine if it's worth it to you. When I first started freelancing, we moved from a two-bedroom apartment to a one-bedroom apartment to save a few hundred dollars a month. It was a tight squeeze to not have an office to work in, but we made the best of the situation and ultimately were able to make the shift to full-time freelancing much easier.

The same is true of other expenses like car payments. Downgrading might be a quick and easy way to eliminate an expense that costs most people hundreds of dollars a month. If you can trade in your expensive car for a less pricey model, you might even be able to eliminate a vehicle payment altogether. Electricity is another less obvious place where you can cut back on your spending. In the summer, you can bump the thermostat up a few degrees so the air conditioner doesn't need to run as frequently, and do the opposite in the winter. Yes, you may have to wear a sweater in the cold months but it could save you $50 per month – which adds up when every penny counts in your freelancing budget!

In other words, get creative with ways you can save money on your expenses. Even fixed costs don't necessarily have to be fixed. Everyone has bills to pay, but you can be smart about what you pay and prioritize the items that truly matter to you. Everything else can merely be downgraded to a lesser spending category until you can achieve a full-time income from your freelancing. When you do reach that exciting point where freelancing more than covers your bills, you can always ease up on the budget. That being said, most people decide to stick with budgeting because they like knowing that their expenses are kept low. It reassures them they have enough to take care of unexpected bills and covers them in case of a business famine, and that is a priceless gift.

Taxes

WE TALKED IN PART ONE about how much you might owe in taxes, but now is the time to ensure that you set aside enough money to actually cover those costs. The amount owed will vary based on your business structure, the amount you pay yourself, and your overall income for the year. Once you have an idea of how much you need to earn to cover your expenses (including debt, which we'll cover in the next section), you need to add a certain percentage over that amount for your taxes. Sole proprietors, partners, and LLCs will all need to cough up that 15.3 percent tax designed for the self-employed.

In addition to that, you also have your income tax bracket which depends on your filing status and taxable income. For 2023, here is what you can expect your tax bracket to be:

Tax Rate	Single	Married Filing Jointly	Married Filing Separately	Head of Household
10%	$0 to $11,000	$0 to $22,000	$0 to $11,000	$0 to $15,700
12%	$11,001 to $44,725	$22,001 to $89,450	$11,001 to $44,725	$15,701-$59,850
22%	$44,726 to $95,375	$89,451 to $190,750	$44,726 to $95,375	$59,851 to $95,350
24%	$95,376 to $182,100	$190,751 to $364,200	$95,376 to $182,100	$95,351 to $182,100
32%	$182,101 to $231,250	$364,201 to $462,500	$182,101 to $231,250	$182,101 to $231,250
35%	$231,251 to $578,125	$462,501 to $693,750	$231,251 to $346,875	$231,251 to $578,100
37%	$578,126+	$693,751+	$346,876+	$578,101+

This is where it can help to forecast the numbers you intend to make for the year. Once you know how much you will owe in taxes, you can add that to your fixed and variable costs. For example, if you make $60,000 per year and are married and filing jointly, your tax rate will include the 15.3 percent self-employment tax and a 12 percent tax rate. Don't forget to factor this into your budget alongside all of your other expenses. The money you earn is not solely your own but belongs in part to the federal and state governments.

To give you an example, a $60,000 salary will require $9,180 in self-employment taxes and $7,200 in income taxes. If you needed the full $60,000 just to cover your expenses, you would actually need to make roughly $76,380 per year to cover the cost of your taxes and necessary income. Knowing how much you need to make for a feasible budget requires you to do a little planning when it comes to setting your rates. Make sure that the rates you set are reasonable and allow you enough space to earn the money you need to pay your bills without trading your soul or all of your spare time just to make ends meet. While hustling might be a given in the early stages of your career, there are other things that you must consider when it comes to how sustainable this is long-term. You may need to raise your rates if you intend to cover your tax bill and the rest of your bills via self-employment income.

Managing Debt

AS YOU WERE MAKING your budget, you might have come across a category that we haven't talked about much just yet: debt payments. Odds are these fall into your fixed costs if you aren't actively spending money on a credit card. This could include your student loan debt, your car payments, or a home equity line of credit (HELOC). All of these have a recurring sum due at the end of each month and a portion of the sum goes directly to the interest on your debt. It can mean you are essentially throwing money out the window until you get the principal paid down enough to eliminate most of the interest payments. What can you do to manage your debt and keep it from preventing your transition into freelancing?

Here is a quick note before we dive into what you can do about your debt: if you are using your credit cards to cover your basic living expenses like rent, a car payment, or groceries, you need to get your spending under control first. Some people will use their credit cards to give them a longer runway to transition into freelancing, but this isn't the wisest move. Credit cards frequently have excessively high interest rates which will make it that much harder for you to pay them down when you do finally start to make enough to cover your bills. Reliance on credit cards should be an indicator you are not yet ready to make the move into full-time freelancing. Consider getting a part-time job to help cover your living expenses as listed on your budget or cut expenses in variable spending categories. It will require you to be a little stricter with yourself, but it could save you piles of money when you don't have to pay back those astronomical interest rates.

With that out of the way, you should be ready to manage your debt in a new way. The first and perhaps most obvious way to cut back on debt spending is simply to pay it down. There are two major schools of thought on how you can master debt instead of allowing it to control you (and your finances). The first is to pay off your smallest debt first. Then, you take whatever you were paying on the smallest debt and funnel it into the second smallest debt. With both of those paid off, you roll the total payments into the third debt, and so on. Eventually, you will have a huge "snowball" of accumulated payments that go into your biggest debt. The benefit of this method is it allows you to have some quick and easy wins early in the process. You'll eliminate some of the smaller debts, cut back on the number of payments you have each month, and feel that much lighter and freer from your debt.

However, this might not be the right method for you if you have debt with an exorbitant interest rate. List out all of your debts in one column and their corresponding interest rates in the other. Now, sort them by the highest interest rate to the lowest. This will help you to see where to funnel your efforts first. Put every spare dollar you can into the debt with the highest interest rate. When that one is paid off, take the payments and channel them into your debt with the second-highest interest rate, much like you would have done with the snowball method. You'll save more money on interest by tackling them in this order, but it might not give you as many quick wins if your biggest debt is the one that happens to have the highest interest rate.

With both of these methods, you will curtail your savings for a little while in order to get your debt managed. In the end, it is worth this sacrifice because it could trim monthly expenses by a significant number. When your monthly expenses are low, your runway can be much smaller and you will give yourself more time to transition to freelancing full-time while you attempt to find a roster of paying clients. As soon as your debt is paid off or is at a more manageable point, start to funnel money back into your savings account so you have a decent runway to move toward a new career shift. We'll talk more about your savings and runway in the next chapter.

The goal at this stage of budget-setting is two-fold. First, you want to see what your actual expenses are right now and determine where money is likely leaking from your bank account. The only true way to determine where your spending is out of control is by looking at the cold hard facts. It is impossible to lie to yourself about what you spend on dining out or even on your credit card debt when you have your bank statements in front of you. I highly recommend that if you have skipped over these steps, you go back and do them before moving on to the next section about setting up your savings and runway for your transition. Second, this method of budget-setting gives you a good idea of where you can more realistically trim your spending. It allows you to set your priorities, be realistic about what you can and can't stand to cut, and it lets you know just what you will need to earn to cover your expenses with freelancing.

If you need help sticking with your budget, you can always purchase the notebook that serves as a companion to this book. It will give you space to track your spending in each category so you can see where your spending is (or is not) on track. Some people prefer to manage things digitally but a paper record might be easier and more efficient for you. I recommend keeping the notebook in the car or in your bag so you can add expenses as you spend them at the store instead of waiting until the end of the month to tally everything up. This gives you a good idea of when your allotted spending is up for the month instead of waiting until the end of the month and realizing that you are *way* over budget. If you notice that spending is starting to get out of hand in a particular category, you can scale back spending for the rest of the month. Doing so for a few months in a row might mean you need to reevaluate whether your estimated spending numbers are realistic and whether they need to be adjusted.

A budget is a living document that should change with you as you adjust to new spending habits and a fluctuating income. Don't feel like your budget has to be set in stone. Instead, you can revisit these exercises every few months to ensure you keep up with your spending habits. If your spending is under control and you find your budget is easy to stick to, I still recommend revisiting it annually to see if there are new areas where you can trim expenses further while managing to live a life that brings you joy. It can turn into a fun game where you see just how much you can save in new categories. For some people, it even sparks new hobbies. For example, you might want to cut out your restaurant budget and learn to cook gourmet meals at home.

It's important to mention at this point that you don't want your budget to feel as though you are massively depriving yourself of the things that bring you joy. If you look at your budget and feel as though you can never enjoy the finer things in life again, you might be going into it with the wrong attitude. While you may not be able to shop as much as you used to or go out with friends as frequently, you can add a line item in to your budget for saving for some of these special occasions. We'll talk about that in the next chapter on savings. Keep in mind you are making a commitment to stick to a budget for a real purpose: namely, your own happiness with your career. Freelancing has the potential to be quite lucrative once you get the business off the ground. It offers you more flexibility than an office job, allows you to put your skills to good use, and gives you the freedom to scale your income and your business operations. You might need to adjust your mindset toward freelancing before you can make the move to financial planning for the career shift, which we cover in my *Freelance Freedom* book.

With all of that being said, it's time to look at one of the most crucial pieces of your budget when you make the transition to freelancing: your savings account. Let's dive right in and see what you need to do to get your business off the ground.

Did you know that the majority of Americans couldn't pay an unexpected $1,000 bill if it came in the mail? Maybe you need a new set of tires, your child broke his arm falling off the jungle gym, or you had a broken window in your living room. An unexpected bill is just that – something you can't anticipate arriving. The question is: are you prepared to weather that kind of financial storm, especially if you make the move into freelancing full-time? Think long and hard about whether you are financially prepared to leave your nine-to-five in hopes of making it as a freelancer. It all starts with making sure you have some money in the bank that gives you peace of mind so you can focus fully on your career move.

Picture what it will be like when you feel ready to move into freelancing full-time. You can almost picture the flexibility it allows for in your schedule, allowing you to wake up early and start hustling so you can be off work when your kids get home from school. Maybe you just want to be able to enjoy a leisurely cup of coffee in the middle of the afternoon without being tied down to a cubicle. There is something appealing to you about this lifestyle. Bring up a picture of what it is in your mind's eye.

Now, I want you to think a step further. What would it look like to feel as though you were free to enjoy those moments? What would it feel like to know you had the time and energy to devote to your work without overworking in an attempt to pay the bills? Without a savings account in place, finances are likely to be at the forefront of your mind every hour of every day. You need to hustle to get more jobs just to cover the mortgage. Maybe that means you need to work around the clock, which will only end up in burnout instead of the freedom and flexibility you desired when you first decided to embrace this new and unique career path. Stress over finances can ruin every good thing about your upcoming shift, but it doesn't have to be that way.

Once you make the commitment to freelancing, there are a few things you need to do to ensure you have the capacity to focus on building a career you love. All of them relate to your financial mindset and your savings account. We'll start by looking at your runway and finish by looking at how you can implement savings into your regular routine.

Runway

WHEN YOU THINK ABOUT starting a freelancing career, you need a little bit of breathing room for your finances. To me, that means you need to have a savings account that offers you a little bit of runway. Consider the image of a plane taking off. The pilot can't automatically tilt up the nose of the plane and put it in the sky. Instead, it needs a little bit of room to accelerate and build up momentum before it can launch into the sky. The same is true of your freelancing career. Deciding to quit your job in a fit of passion one day is a bad idea unless you know you have the financial preparation to weather the storms freelancing can bring.

Starting your business from scratch is an inevitable famine situation. If you haven't worked to build up a few small clients while working your day job, it will place that much more pressure on you financially if you decide to make the shift without planning. However, some people really don't have the option of grinding on a freelancing side hustle while they work full-time. Maybe you already put in long hours at the office or you have kids at home who need your presence. There are tons of reasons why you might not be able to transition into freelancing the slow way. Even if you can do things slowly, you need a runway to get you started.

A runway is a specific time period during which you will pursue your freelancing full-time without having to worry about your financial obligations. I usually recommend a savings of three to six months tucked away inside an emergency fund. The longer you can maintain your lifestyle (which has already been pared down in the previous chapter), the better you will be able to focus on building a business rather than how your rent will get paid.

Perhaps this sounds like an unrealistic goal for you because you don't make much at your current job. Freelancing appeals to many people because it offers a generous wage for skills only you can provide. If your day job doesn't offer fair pay for the work you do and you struggle to have money left over at the end of every month to put back in savings, it might be time to shift to a different career move. For example, you might want to pick up a part-time job to cover half of your living expenses while you spend the rest of your hours building up a docket of clients as quickly as you can so you can leave the rat race behind for good.

Of course, there comes a time when your runway might start to run out. This is where it's crucial to know what your plan is when the time arrives. Let's look at a few scenarios that might arise when you make the transition:

Scenario 1:

You have been working steadily at freelancing for four months of your six-month runway. You still haven't started earning enough to cover your living expenses and you are worried about money running out.

Sometimes, building a business happens slowly. If you have been at this for a while without seeing the traction you need to pay your bills, you really have two options. One: you could double down on your freelancing career. This might mean exploring new job boards, cold-calling clients you could work with locally, or simply putting in more proposals. It would mean less flexible work time and could even mean you work more than forty hours each week simply trying to make ends meet. One thing to keep in mind is this hustle-and-grind method is only meant to be temporary. If you find that you are putting in fifty- or sixty-hour weeks for months on end, it might be time to reevaluate your approach.

Two: you might want to consider getting a part-time job to give you the flexibility to pursue freelancing on a full-time basis. This might be something in the field where you have some experience or it could even be a minimum wage job that requires very little of you mentally or emotionally. If you have two months of runway left, you can stretch that to four months with a part-time job that covers half of your living expenses. A part-time job gives you flexibility to work around it without having to stay up all night to get your freelancing work done. If you're seeing a little bit of traction with your freelancing career, this might be the smarter move.

Scenario 2:

You have exhausted your runway and are now strapped for cash. You have made some traction on your freelancing career and don't want to backpedal to a day job when you feel that success is just around the corner.

Eventually, even the most generous runway is going to be depleted if work doesn't pick up fast enough. We covered what you can do if you're getting close to the end of your runway in the first scenario, so let's approach this one from a different angle. Let's say that your runway is completely tapped out, but you do have a few clients who are contributing to your overall income. It comes close to the ability to pay your bills entirely on what you're earning, but it isn't quite enough to do so with ease. If you were to go back to a day job, you would lose the clients you already have due to a lack of time. You know that success with your freelancing career is coming, so what can you do to prolong the amount of time you spend investing in this career shift?

You could consider whether you have any other financial resources you can tap into to help bridge the gap. For example, you may be able to take a loan against your retirement savings account or put your monthly necessities on a credit card with a no-interest rate introductory period. Many people have financial resources at their disposal beyond their emergency fund. If you truly believe that your freelancing career is about to pay off because you have clients who are satisfied with your work and have built up a great portfolio for yourself, then betting on yourself might be the next right thing for you.

Of course, there comes a time when you may have to embrace that you need some financial help when it comes to pursuing your freelancing career. Before you embark on a freelancing path, make sure you clearly outline what your next steps are when the runway is depleted (just in case you ever get there). Your list might look something like this:

1. Save six months of expenses covered by a runway or emergency fund.
2. Cash out my retirement account.
3. Put variable living expenses on a credit card.

Once you get to a certain point on the list, note when you will start to consider looking for at least part-time work. For me, it would be the point at which I had to cash out my retirement savings. I might want to give freelancing my absolute best, but there comes a point when you have to realize you are putting your future in jeopardy over this dream. That doesn't necessarily mean a career change isn't in the cards for you, but it might mean you need to proceed more slowly with a handful of clients while you work on your reputation, testimonials, and client interactions.

Getting a part-time job to supplement what you earn via freelancing is *not* admitting defeat or failure with the process. It gives you the space, freedom, and flexibility to pursue your dream without the stress of wondering how you will pay your bills. While doubling down on your career might be a smart move at this point, it might not be enough. Maybe you need a change of pace to unlock the freedom you need to make this career work for you.

Scenario 3:

You depleted your emergency fund and runway, but you finally have enough freelancing clients to cover the bills.

Last but not least, what do you do if you finally have enough freelancing clients to pay the bills? The first thing you need to do is celebrate your major accomplishment! The next is evaluate what remains of your emergency fund or runway account. Your financial stresses aren't over just because you had a good month that covered your living expenses. Freelancing remains a feast or famine type of business, so you should carefully consider your savings account a few months into your freelancing journey. If you have enough work to cover the bills but have no savings remaining in the backup account, it's time to think about setting more money in savings again.

This might mean you need to hustle a little harder at your freelancing gig. Sure, you are making enough to pay your bills but you don't have anything extra left over at the end of the month. You need to pick up an extra project or two in order to contribute to your savings accounts and restore the money you depleted in your pursuit of freelancing. Yes, you may have to work a little harder for a while. However, you still have far more freedom and flexibility than you had at your day job. We'll look at some methods for setting money aside in savings in the next section. The same methods apply whether you are looking to build up your runway for the first time or need to replenish it after a lean financial season.

Setting Aside Savings

ALL OF THIS TALK ABOUT runways and emergency funds is great, but how do you actually make one? I have good news and bad news for you about how savings work. The good news is saving may be easier than you think – and you have a lot of control over how this account grows. The bad news is it takes time, sometimes more time than you may anticipate. Especially if you are trying to build your runway to six months of living expenses to cover your transition to freelancing, this isn't something you can likely build overnight.

First, let's talk about how you can grow your savings account. The first and most obvious way to start putting money aside for your future is to examine your budget. If you are following along, you already have a basic framework for your budget. You have an idea of what your variable expenses are as well as your fixed costs. You may even be getting a handle on your debt so you can free up additional money that can be funneled into your savings account. The question is: how much can you save each month?

Chances are that it's unrealistic for you to save a full month of living expenses each month unless you are great at living below your means and have a sizable income at your day job. Instead, you need to see how much is reasonable for you to set aside in a savings account. This is actually easier than it sounds. First, start with how much money you have coming in each month (use your net income, the amount that actually hits your bank account on payday). Write that at the top of the page, front and center. Now, tally up your fixed and variable expenses to see how much you're spending. Write that underneath and subtract it from your net income to see how much you have left over. This "leftover" amount is *not* there for you to spend on frivolous items, entertainment, or new clothes. This is the amount you can move directly into your savings account.

What do you do if your expenses are higher than your income? This is a major problem that needs to be addressed immediately. This means you are not just living for your paycheck but that you are living well above your means. You might frequently overdraft your bank account, borrow money from others, and find yourself strapped when unexpected expenses pop up – and they will! This is the time to slash some of those variable expenses. It might feel painful at first to have to tell your friends you can't go out with them, to cut those shopping sprees on Friday nights, and to pack your lunch to take to the office with you. If you can, try cutting your fixed expenses down by disconnecting your cable, buying a less expensive car, or paying down debt. Do whatever it takes to make it so that you have some money left over at the end of the month or you will never truly have the freedom to pursue a major career move.

A deficit in your budget might also be a sign you need to do more to bring in additional income rather than slashing expenses. This is a viable solution as well, but you will have to come to terms with the fact you need to work a little harder. If you don't buy in to hustle culture, it could be almost painful to think about working above and beyond your full-time gig. Fortunately, you have a couple of options for how you can boost your income. First, you could pick up a part-time job that uses the same skills you use at your day job. If you're an assistant or a secretary right now, you might be a receptionist for a different business in the evenings. Alternatively, you could start your freelancing career and pick up a client or two to supplement your income. You can work these jobs at your leisure (as long as the work gets done on time). This allows you to start building up your reputation, gaining experience, and earning a little extra cash. It might be less stable than a part-time office job, but it might work out better for you.

With that out of the way, let's shift our attention back to how you can save more money. I will assume you have some money left over after you pay your expenses. Let's suppose you have $500 left over at the end of the month. You know you have this money left over and you need to do some very specific things to keep it safe from frivolous spending. Without taking a few precautions, the money can easily filter out of your bank account on a new outfit or too many lattes when you have to work through the afternoon slump. There are two major techniques you can use to protect that money: paying yourself first and opening a separate banking account.

I want you to treat your savings as if it was a bill you had to pay. In many ways, it *is* a bill you need to pay if you want to transition to doing something other than what you're committed to right now. When your paycheck hits your bank account, you are already used to paying your bills with it. You funnel some to your rent, your electric bill, and take the rest to go grocery shopping. If you're lucky, you have some money left in your account once all of the "necessities" are bought and paid for. This is the wrong approach and will result in a lackluster savings account. Instead, I want you to think of your savings the same way you view your rent: a non-negotiable expense. As soon as your paycheck hits your account, take the amount that you have earmarked for savings and pay yourself.

Stop thinking of your savings as something nice to have if there's anything left at the end of the month. It should be your first and highest priority, especially if you don't have any type of emergency fund in place or if you want to make a major career transition. Take the money you want to save directly out of your bank account without even thinking about it. Better yet, set up an automatic transfer on each of your paydays to prevent you from forgetting about it, spending it, or allocating it to something else that doesn't matter. You can always adjust your other spending habits to accommodate your increased savings. Variable expenses can be slashed in favor of saving. It might mean you eat more rice and beans than you normally would, but it will be worth it when you see those savings rack up. Every meal you sacrifice or every shirt you put back on the rack brings you that much closer to your goal. It can be a rewarding experience to reframe spending so it allows you to look at what you *gain* instead of what you have to *sacrifice*. Pay yourself first and you will know exactly what you have left to spend in other categories.

Second, you need to set yourself up for success with your savings account. This means you do actually need a dedicated savings account rather than just hoping that you can leave the money in your checking account without spending it. This money will likely filter out of your checking account because it's easy to swipe your debit card, knowing there's a few hundred or thousand dollars extra in the account. It makes your savings murkier and makes it more challenging for you to know whether you have hit your goal and can leave your day job. Always open up a separate account so that you can reach toward your financial goals.

If you have multiple goals, I would recommend setting up a savings account for each one. For example, let's say you need your runway as well as a new laptop and software specific to the work you want to do. Open an account for your runway and pay yourself first into this account. Set aside a small sum of money for your business equipment in another savings account each time you get paid. Decide in advance what percentage of your savings amount goes to each account and automate those transfers if you can. It becomes crystal clear when you hit your goal because you don't have any other expenses coming out of these accounts.

Along with this idea of having separate accounts, it's also advisable to open these accounts somewhere other than your primary bank. In fact, you should open your savings account where it would be inconvenient for you to go pull funds out or swap money around between your accounts. If you open a savings account at your primary bank, you might find it extremely easy to swap funds from one account to another. All it takes is a few clicks and a few seconds. When you want to spend something on an item that is mostly frivolous to you, it's far too easy. Instead, you should keep your savings accounts at a different branch on the opposite side of town. You can even open up a savings account online (as long as it's an FDIC-insured bank).

This is also a great time to plug being savvy with your money moves. Look for a savings account that bears interest, particularly high-yield savings accounts. While your money rests on its laurels, you can earn interest that makes your savings account grow. The benefit of these accounts is they're still highly liquid, meaning you can withdraw your funds whenever you want to. Unlike other interest-bearing savings methods like certificates of deposit (CDs), you don't have to keep it in the account for specific period of time in order to capitalize on the interest. However, it still works harder for you than a traditional savings account that may not earn anything. It's a way to put your money to work for you while you wait to put it in use when you make the transition to freelancing.

Are you tired of thinking about your runway altogether at this point? It's frustrating that it may take you months or even a year to put together a runway that could support you for six months while you hustle to get freelancing clients. But think of how rewarding it would feel to know you could pursue your dreams without fear of the financial future. If you have a well-paying job right now, you might choose to look at it through the lens of finishing a "sentence" in your current role. There are times when you have to stick with something you don't love in order to have flexibility to more fully pursue your dreams at a future date.

Keep in mind: staying at your day job isn't a forever thing. You slog through the endless days a little easier knowing there's an end in sight. Spend some time figuring out how much you can save and how long it will take you to fund that runway account. This is all the time you need to dedicate to your job and you can start to cross each day off on the calendar as you move one step closer to your dream of freelancing and doing what you love in a way that feels life-giving to you instead of draining. Every single day brings you closer to that dream if you can stick with the strategies found here to bolster your savings account.

Alternatively, you could slash your necessary runway in half by committing to working a reliable job part-time while you pursue freelancing. If you absolutely hate your current job and the idea of staying there for another year fills you with dread, be willing to pivot. You could take on a different job that supplements your income and gives you a little bit of freedom to start growing your freelancing career. You can work early mornings as a barista or late nights at 24-hour gym. A little bit of money rolling in is better than nothing and can help you bridge the gap between a day job you hate and a freelancing career you'll love.

Managing Your Money

With some basic framework laid for your expenses and savings, it's time to talk about how to best manage your money in each category. There is some serious flexibility regarding how you keep track of your expenses, so we'll cover a few of the most popular methods here. The important thing is you find a creative way to manage your spending, namely your variable expenses. How do you make sure you aren't spending more than you allotted on your expenses from month to month?

The first and easiest thing you can do is stick to a cash system. When your paycheck hits your account, pay yourself first and place that money into your savings account like we covered in the last chapter. From here, you can start to pull out money that belongs to other categories. Get cash for your grocery budget, entertainment budget, restaurant budget, and so on. If you have an expense that varies from month to month, you should have already set the amount you *want* to spend on that category. Give it a cash budget by putting the money you plan to spend in each one into an envelope, a divider in your wallet, or some other system that separates your funds from the rest of your money. The benefit to this system is you have a clear idea of how much money you have left to spend in each category.

Another benefit to this system (sometimes referred to as the envelope system) is you are limited to what you can spend because you have a specific allotment of cash. You can't go over what you have to spend simply by swiping your debit card at the checkout. Once the money in the envelope runs out, there is no more money for spending on that category. You can't borrow money from one envelope to another, whereas you could "borrow" money from one category to another if everything is sitting in the same account. You will always be more mindful of what you have to spend because you wouldn't want to get to the register or the end of a meal and realize you don't have enough to pay the bill.

This is also a great way to eliminate your debt. Leave your plastic at home so it won't tempt you to swipe it at the register. Instead, you can focus on paying down your debt rather than racking up more just because you have a hard time sticking to the budget you set in advance. If you find you have a hard time with this envelope system after a few months, it might be time to reevaluate your budget. It might be unrealistic for you to spend $50 or less on restaurant spending if you work a variable schedule or prioritize nights out with your friends. Maybe you can assign more money to this category and take it from somewhere else (not your savings account though!). You can take the money from your grocery budget or other entertainment to bolster the areas that you love spending most.

Some people just can't get behind the idea of paying cash for everything. Carrying around hundreds in cash can feel risky, and most places prefer you to swipe your plastic instead of using cash. Either way, you need a system to track how much you're spending and where that money is going. Technology like You Need a Budget is a great way to categorize expenses. It integrates with your online bank account portal and allows you to assign a category to your spending. All you have to do is open the app when you get to the car and select a category for the money you just spent. It automatically keeps track of your spending in every area which can keep you on track without giving up your debit or credit card. It does come with a small monthly fee, but it might be preferable instead of keeping track of things using the paper and pen method.

Of course, you *can* use paper and pen to detail your spending. My notebook will give you a space to write down every receipt that you incur so that you can add up what you spend on groceries, clothing, and other items that come up month after month. It's small enough to tuck into your glovebox in your car or in your bag. There's nothing complex about writing down what you spend. Think of it in the same way that you might keep a food log when trying to lose a little bit of weight. You only write down what you spend. Chances are that you'll start to think twice about spending money if you know you'll have to write it down in your book when all is said and done. It might be just enough to give you pause about whether that purchase is worthwhile or whether you'll regret spending your limited funds later on.

Keep in mind that there will be some degree of sacrifice when you start to budget. If you have never tried to rein in your spending before, it will feel uncomfortable and restrictive to budget this way. Try to view it as if you were playing a game like Monopoly. How much money can you allot to your spending and how can you get creative to keep it under that number? At the end of the month, anything you *didn't* spend can be funneled into your savings account. This is a nice bonus that can help you move the needle forward on your savings and inch you ever closer to your goal of being able to leave your day job.

Are You Ready to Quit Your Day Job?

Maybe you have already done the mindset work to prepare you for freelancing (if you haven't, be sure to see the first book in this series). Now, you have some of the groundwork laid to get your finances under control before you leap into the feast or famine scenario that accompanies most freelancing work. You have a budget working for you and you have a runway that will support you in the first few months of moving into freelancing as a day job. Are you *really* ready to quit your day job to transition to freelancing?

If you have been following along with the exercises in this book, then you might be totally ready to dive into freelancing. Only you can tell whether you're financially prepared to make your move into freelancing. The answer isn't as clear-cut as most people would like. There are no hard and fast rules about having $10,000 in savings or a certain number of clients lined up. Instead, the answers depend on your comfort level as well as your financial preparedness. Let's take a look at each of these criteria in turn to see if you feel ready to make this huge leap into doing something you love and leaving the day job that might be sucking your soul.

One of the first questions you need to ask yourself is how much uncertainty you can tolerate before you make the move. Some people may not want to transition to freelancing until they know that they love the work and the schedule. The only way to truly know if you love it more than your day job is to simply get started. Pick up a client or two in your spare time to see if you like it as much as you thought you would. Yes, you will have to sacrifice time in the early morning or late-night hours to make this work alongside a demanding day job. If you have a hard time facing down the uncertainty of whether you will *really* like this more than your day job, there is no better test than to simply get a few clients and try it out.

Maybe your concern is more centered around the flux in income that comes from a career move. Moving into a new career and not knowing when you will have a paycheck coming in for the foreseeable future is scary. If you haven't yet gotten your feet wet with freelancing, now might be the time to try taking on a client or two. This gives you a small amount of income you can count on and minimizes the size of your runway that you need to have before taking the plunge. It offers a little more stability when making the transition. You won't go from working a nine-to-five right into having nothing to do but hustle. You'll have some work you need to get done and can focus the remaining time into getting more clients.

The real issue that people have surrounding leaving their day job is their degree of financial preparedness. When you have a solid emergency fund built up for your expenses, it might be time to leave your day job. On the other hand, those who have no idea how they will make ends meet and are relying on each paycheck to cover their bills might not be ready for the financial onslaught of bills that are bound to crop up. As soon as you think you might be in the clear, odds are an unexpected expense is going to pop up whether it is something medical, something for your kids, or an increase in your rent. Without some degree of financial preparedness, you will flounder in the sea of upcoming bills and start racking up debt simply to cover the bare necessities.

Being ready to quit your day job means that you have laid the groundwork for a successful business – because it *should* be more than a hobby to you at this point. You need to select a business structure that works for you, set realistic goals for your income, and take care of the minutiae that accompany running a business. Once you have a handle on your personal finances and a clear goal for where you are headed in your business, you might feel comfortable and confident enough to make freelancing your day job. It's time to start learning how to command top dollar for your services and how to communicate with clients to achieve those goals, as we'll see in the next book in this series.

www.ingramcontent.com/pod-product-compliance
Lightning Source LLC
Chambersburg PA
CBHW061331120726

48001CB00002B/804